Saving Wildlife

Rufus Bellamy

First published in 2004 by Franklin Watts
96 Leonard Street, London EC2A 4XD

Franklin Watts Australia
45-51 Huntley Street, Alexandria NSW 2015

Editor: Adrian Cole, Design: Proof Books,
Art Director: Jonathan Hair, Picture Researcher:
Kathy Lockley

Acknowledgements
ACO Wildlife, a division of ACO Technologies plc 18 b.
© Animals Asia Foundation/www:animals asia.org 23 b.
ARS, USDA /Photo by Keith Weller 6 /Photo by Scott Bauer
21 b. Jon Bower/Ecoscene 20. Mike Brossley/WDCS 5. Mark
Carwadine/Still Pictures Cover tr, 27. Manfred
Danegger/N.H.P.A. Cover tl. Nigel J. Dennis/N.H.P.A. 28.
© Digital Vision Ltd. All rights reserved 14, 16, 22. Ron
Giling/Still Pictures 11. Greenpeace/Eric Algra 17 b, /Gavin
Newman 21 t. © Stichting Greenpeace Council 21tl.
Martin Harvey/Still Pictures 19 t, 23t. Martin
Harvey/N.H.P.A. 13 t, 25t. Hellio & Van Ingen/N.H.P.A. 19
b. ITDG/Jon Hellin 17 t. Frans Lemmens/Still Pictures 9.
David Lucas 4. Eero Murtomaki/N.H.P.A. 7 b. Gilles
Nicolet/Still Pictures 2, 12. Robert Pickett/Ecoscene 25 b.
Heinz Plenge/ Still Pictures 1, 8. Alain Pons/Still Pictures
Cover b, 13 b. Rex Features 24. Ray Roberts/Ecoscene 29.
© Save-the-Rhino 7 t, 31. Michael Sewell/Still Pictures 15.
©Alan Watson/Forest Light 10. WWF-Canon /Susan A.
MAINKA 26.

Published in the United States by Smart Apple Media
2140 Howard Drive West, North Mankato,
Minnesota 56003

Library of Congress Cataloging-in-Publication Data

Bellamy, Rufus.
Saving wildlife / by Rufus Bellamy.
p. cm. — (Action for the environment)
Includes index.
ISBN 1-58340-596-8
1. Wildlife conservation—Juvenile literature. I. Title.
II. Series.

QL83.B46 2005
333.95'416—dc22   2004059197

9 8 7 6 5 4 3 2 1

Contents

Wildlife in danger

There are millions of different types—or species—of plants and animals in the world. Some of these species are threatened or endangered because they exist in such small numbers that they could easily die out altogether and become extinct.

EXTINCTION IS FOREVER

Many species have already become extinct. For example, some scientists believe dinosaurs became extinct because of severe changes in Earth's climate. Today, many animals face extinction because people hunt them or destroy the places where they live—their habitats. This has happened to the tiger: only about 6,000 tigers now remain in the wild—between 5 and 10 percent of the number that existed in the 1900s.

A young gorilla. Gorillas are one of the most endangered animals in the world. If more is not done to protect them in the wild, they could soon exist only in zoos.

SAVING WILDLIFE AROUND THE WORLD

Around the world, people are working to protect plants and animals. There are many projects that effectively protect endangered wildlife and allow plants and animals to reproduce successfully. Unfortunately, many species remain in danger, and there is a lot of work left to do.

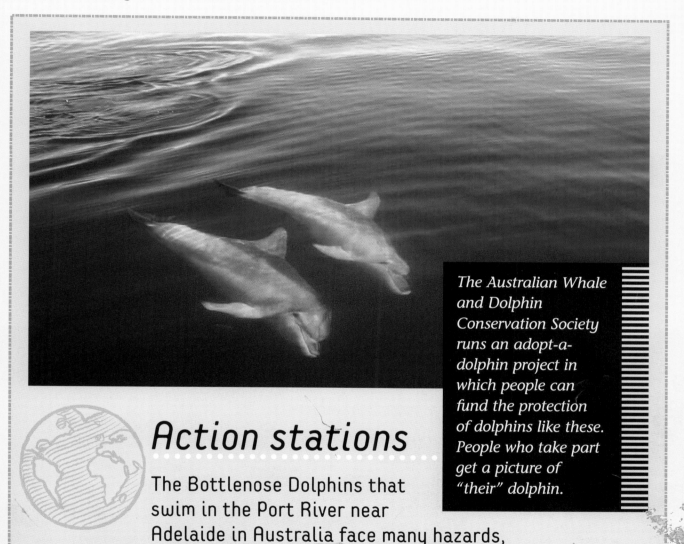

The Australian Whale and Dolphin Conservation Society runs an adopt-a-dolphin project in which people can fund the protection of dolphins like these. People who take part get a picture of "their" dolphin.

Action stations

The Bottlenose Dolphins that swim in the Port River near Adelaide in Australia face many hazards, including motorboats, garbage, and pollution. To help save these animals, laws are being passed to create a sanctuary that will protect them. However, campaigners, including the Whale and Dolphin Conservation Society, say that even stronger laws are needed to ensure a safe future for these intelligent animals.

Why protect species?

All living things—including humans—depend on other animals and plants to survive. Therefore, it is important to give all species as much protection as possible—even ugly-looking insects!

FOOD CHAINS

Plants and animals are linked together in food chains. If one species is lost, then the species that are linked to it suffer. For example, if farm chemicals kill the flowers and insects in a field, there is less food for birds. Bird numbers might drop as a result. If a species becomes extinct, the impact on other species can be devastating.

Unfortunately, many human activities, such as modern farming, reduce the number of different species in a particular area.

SAVE THE . . .

Many campaigns to save wildlife focus on one particular species, such as the rhinoceros, whale, or elephant. These animals attract a lot of public interest, and many people are willing to give money to help them. This money is often used to protect the habitats in which these animals live, which also helps the other species that live there.

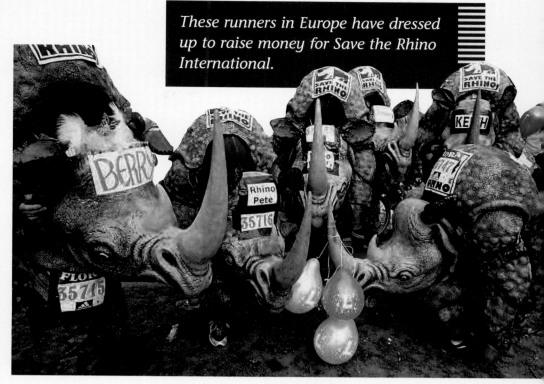

These runners in Europe have dressed up to raise money for Save the Rhino International.

Action stations

The white-tailed sea eagle lives near water in the Baltic region of Europe, where it hunts for fish. In the 1970s, man-made chemical pollutants (mainly from farming and manufacturing) poisoned the fish. The eagles ate the fish, were poisoned, and began to have fewer young. Most of the damaging pollutants have now been banned, and the World Wildlife Fund (WWF) has provided the eagles with nontoxic food and protected nest sites. As a result, the number of white-tailed sea eagles in the area is rising slowly.

The plight of the white-tailed sea eagle shows how different species are dependent on each other. It also shows that most living things need a clean and healthy environment in order to survive.

7

Safe havens

The biggest threat to wildlife is the destruction of the places where plants and animals live. For example, giant pandas are endangered because more than half of the bamboo forests that they depend on have been destroyed.

SURVIVAL SPACES

In many countries, plants and animals are conserved in special protected areas. These areas range in size from small nature reserves to enormous national parks. In Peru, the Tambopata Reserve covers more than 3.7 million acres (1.5 million ha). It is home to tens of thousands of species of plants and animals, including rare orchids, giant otters, anacondas, and jaguars.

The Tambopata Reserve is home to the rare jaguar. Despite being protected, the reserve is still threatened by human activity.

DO NOT DISTURB

Tourists visit many protected areas to see the wildlife. It is important that visitors do not disturb the plants or animals they see, so most parks have strict rules. In the Great Barrier Reef Marine Park in Australia, divers are not allowed to take any coral or damage the reef with boat anchors. New eco-working vacations are also organized in many countries, during which visitors can take part in conservation work.

Action stations

The Kruger National Park in South Africa is home to five of the most well-known animals in Africa: lions, elephants, leopards, buffalo, and rhinoceroses. Elephants breed so successfully in the park that they have had to be culled in the past because there was not enough room for them all. Park staff are now experimenting with ways to stop the elephants from breeding so quickly.

An elephant crossing a road in the Kruger National Park. To help deal with increasing numbers of elephants, the park is being linked with other protected areas.

Helping habitats

Habitats around the world are threatened by pressures such as building, logging, pollution, and farming. Problems even affect many protected areas, where people kill animals and harvest plants illegally.

This volunteer in Scotland is planting trees to help restore the country's wildlife.

RESTORING HABITATS

In many places where plant and animal habitats have been destroyed, people are working to restore or re-create what has been lost. In Scotland, a group of volunteers called Trees for Life is replanting hundreds of thousands of Scotch pines. They want to restore part of the ancient Caledonian Forest that used to cover much of the Highlands.

SOWING SEEDS FOR THE FUTURE

Modern farming is a major threat to many species because it destroys important habitats such as wildflower meadows. Now, however, an increasing number of environmentally aware farmers and other groups are planting trees and hedges and sowing wildflower seeds. This will encourage birds, insects, and other wildlife back into the countryside.

Harvesting edible roots from the rain forest. People can use the forest without endangering wildlife.

Action stations

One of the biggest causes of species loss is the destruction of tropical rain forests for timber or agricultural land. But in parts of the Amazon Rain Forest in Brazil, people are using the forest in a way that does not endanger the plants and animals it contains. They collect and sell products such as Brazil nuts and medicinal oils that can be harvested from the forest without chopping it down.

Stop the killing

Many animals are hunted or trapped for their meat, skin, fur, or other parts. For example, rhinoceroses are hunted for their horns, which are turned into powder and used in medicines. This killing has forced many animals to the brink of extinction.

Teachers take a group of school children on a tour of the Korup Rain Forest in Cameroon. Educational projects like this help to keep children from becoming the collectors and poachers of the future.

COLLECTORS AND POACHERS

In many countries, there are laws to stop people from collecting or poaching endangered wildlife. The collection and hunting of other less-threatened plants and animals is also carefully controlled so that they will not become endangered. Unfortunately, poverty and greed still drive people to make money by collecting plants and killing animals illegally.

GUARDS AND EDUCATION

To keep plants and animals from being killed, many nature reserves employ guards. They work to protect wildlife from poachers, who are often armed. However, guards cannot protect all wildlife. Educational projects offer another solution. They can help people understand why wildlife is important and encourage them to get involved in conservation.

In many countries, poaching is bringing some species close to extinction, despite the best efforts of wildlife wardens and guards.

Action stations

Tigers are a protected species; however, medicines made from tiger bones can be sold for a lot of money. As a result, tigers are hunted illegally. In India, guards protect the main national parks where many tigers live. To provide a longer-term solution in these parks, "ecotourism" projects that benefit local people have also been set up. This makes it more likely that they will help conserve the tigers rather than hunt them.

Corbett National Park in India is home to many tigers, such as this one, and is protected by guards. However, even here, poachers still manage to kill these magnificent animals.

13

Stop the trade

One way to save endangered plants and animals is to stop people from buying and selling them or products made from them. If this happens, there will be no money to be made from illegal hunting or plant collecting.

BANNING THE TRADE

CITES (The Convention on International Trade in Endangered Species of Wild Fauna and Flora) is a major international law that bans worldwide trade in more than 800 species of endangered animals, such as whales and rhinoceroses, and plants, such as rare orchids. Every year, police and customs officers, with the help of environmental investigators, arrest people for smuggling banned wildlife products and stop people from selling them.

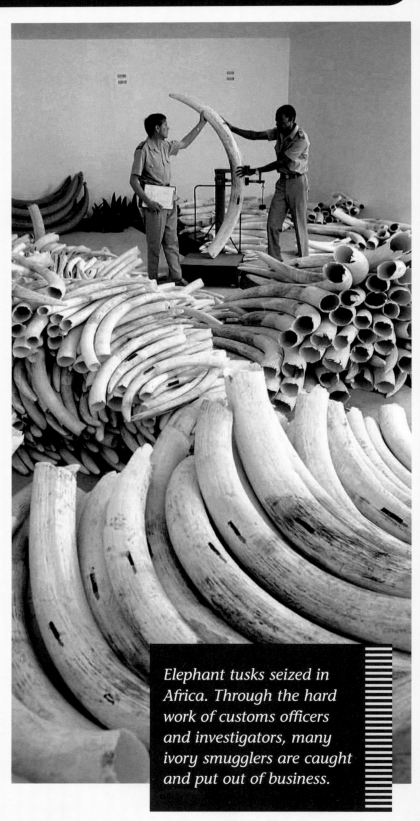

Elephant tusks seized in Africa. Through the hard work of customs officers and investigators, many ivory smugglers are caught and put out of business.

CHANGING TRADITIONS

Educating people is another way to stop the trade in endangered species. Many animals are killed because parts of them are used in traditional medicine. This happens in places such as Southeast Asia. Now, conservation groups are working in countries such as Singapore to show people that alternatives exist.

Action stations

When you are on vacation, you can help to reduce the trade in endangered wildlife. Do not buy things such as shells and coral or anything made from animal parts. At some resorts, you can get your photograph taken with a bear or chimpanzee—these animals have often been illegally captured in the wild, so try not to support this activity.

Although it is nice to bring back a souvenir, do not choose endangered animal products, such as these items made from ivory. Instead, choose something that supports local conservation efforts.

Marine matters

Many fish and other sea creatures are threatened because too many of them have been caught by large fishing fleets around the world. Species that used to be plentiful, such as cod, have dropped significantly in number.

FISHING ACTION

Fish are a vital source of food for many people. Yet, about 70 percent of the world's fish stocks are overfished. Many countries, including those in the European Union, are trying to conserve fish stocks by reducing the size of their fishing fleets. To reduce the impact on other wildlife, such as dolphins, laws have also been introduced to limit the size and type of nets used by fishing boats, as well as the number and type of fish they can catch.

Fishing can harm many marine animals, including dolphins like this one, which get caught in the nets of some fishermen.

MARINE RESERVES

In many countries, conservation groups are working with local people to set up fishery reserves. In these protected areas, fish can breed safely, which will raise fish stock numbers. The Intermediate Technology Development Group (ITDG) is helping several communities in Bangladesh and India.

This pond is part of an ITDG project that aims to "grow" more fish. It is a vital community food source.

Action stations

Blue whales are the largest creatures in the ocean, growing up to 100 feet (30 m) long and weighing about 330,000 pounds (150,000 kg). Many whale species, including blue whales, are endangered, and a lot has been done to protect them—there is a ban on commercial whaling, and a whale sanctuary has been set up in the seas around Antarctica. Despite this fact, many whale species are threatened because they are killed illegally or their feeding grounds are disrupted or polluted. Organizations such as Greenpeace campaign to save whales.

Greenpeace is campaigning for more whale sanctuaries to be set up, including one in the South Pacific.

A helping hand

Many of the things that people do—such as building roads and houses—seriously affect or kill plants and animals. However, there is a lot we can do to help the wildlife that lives around us.

Signs like this warn drivers to slow down because frogs and toads could be crossing the road.

GETTING AROUND SAFELY

Busy places, such as roads, are dangerous and prevent animals from moving around safely. Some roads now have small tunnels underneath them to help animals such as toads cross without getting run over. Other barriers, such as walls, can have small gaps built into them. Man-made dams in rivers can have special channels to allow fish such as salmon to swim upriver to breed.

Tunnels like this help wildlife, including toads and small animals, cross roads safely.

SOMEWHERE TO LIVE AND BREED

Many animals, particularly in cities, cannot easily find a place to live and breed. To help, many people and conservation groups put up bird, bat, or bug boxes or even erect special "tree houses" for owls to live in. Many animals only need peace and quiet. In Turkey, special beaches are set aside in some busy tourist areas so that turtles can lay their eggs undisturbed.

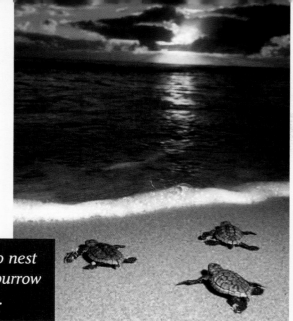

Sea turtles need safe beaches on which to nest because, when they hatch, baby turtles burrow out of the sand and head toward the sea.

Action stations

If you have a garden at home or at school, then you can help give animals a place to live and something to eat. Put out food and water for the birds that visit, and put up a bird box. Sow an area of wildflowers to attract insects, and create a log pile in the shade to provide them with shelter.

This young girl is helping to feed birds in a public park. Parks are often good places to see lots of wildlife, such as rabbits and squirrels.

Pollution cleanup

Human waste, garbage, and other pollution harm and kill plants and animals around the world. Many are poisoned by waste spills or are suffocated by garbage. But people are campaigning to save wildlife by putting a stop to pollution.

CHEMICAL SOUP

Animals such as fish, alligators, and polar bears have been found with cancer and other health problems that are thought to have been caused by man-made chemical pollutants. Among the worst of these are Persistent Organic Pollutants (POPs), which can travel long distances in the air. Now, groups such as Greenpeace and the WWF are calling on governments to pass stricter laws to control these and other polluting chemicals.

Marine litter is just one type of pollution that affects animals. It is estimated that more than one million birds die each year because they eat or are tangled in plastic garbage. Many groups work to clean up areas to stop this from happening.

SAVE OUR CLIMATE

A Greenpeace monitoring station in the Arctic. Air pollution reaches even the polar regions at the top and the bottom of the world.

Action stations

One of the most alarming environmental problems is global warming. Many scientists believe it is caused by "greenhouse" gases, such as carbon dioxide, which are produced mainly by cars and power stations. Earth could warm up by a few degrees in the next 100 years, threatening thousands of species with extinction. Greenpeace is running the "Save Our Climate" campaign so that everyone can help to solve the problem.

GOING ORGANIC

Farm chemicals have caused a large drop in the number of insect and plant species in the countryside. To try to help wildlife, organic farmers have stopped using artificial chemicals. Organic farmers encourage insects that eat pests to come into their fields. These friendly bugs include ladybugs and lacewing larvae.

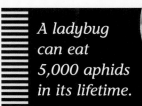

A ladybug can eat 5,000 aphids in its lifetime.

21

Animal rescue

Habitat destruction, pollution, and other man-made problems harm countless animals. In many countries, dedicated teams of people work to rescue and save as many injured animals as possible.

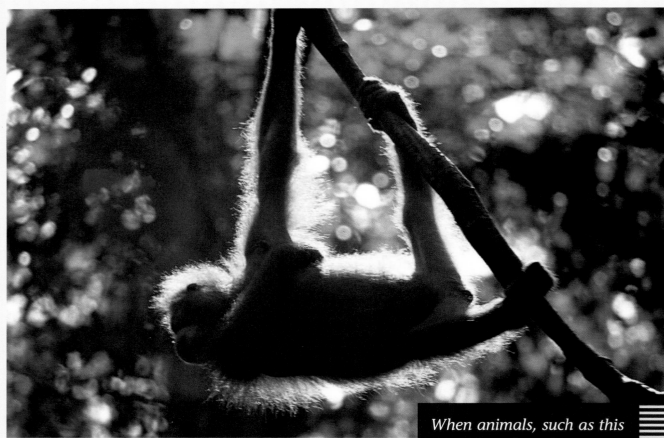

ORANGUTAN HOSPITAL

Around the world, forest fires drive millions of animals from their homes. In Indonesia, this is an especially big problem, and there are a number of sanctuaries that treat and care for injured forest animals. At the Wanariset Center in Kalimantan, for example, orangutans that have been made homeless are treated for injuries or illnesses.

When animals, such as this orangutan, have been nursed back to health at the Wanariset sanctuary, they are released back into protected forest areas.

BIRD CLEANUP

Oil spills poison many marine animals each year. One of the worst spills was the Exxon Valdez disaster in 1989, in which millions of gallons of crude oil polluted water in Prince William Sound in Alaska. Although many thousands of otters and birds died, animal experts and volunteers were able to clean up and save some animals.

Despite the Exxon Valdez tragedy, oil spills still happen today, and volunteers still have to try to save the marine creatures affected.

Action stations

In China, some people use the bile produced by the gallbladders of Asiatic black bears as a medicine. The bears are kept in cruel conditions in cages. To save the bears, a group called the Animals Asia Foundation has worked to free the animals and treat them in a special sanctuary, where they are nursed back to health. So far, the foundation has rescued hundreds of bears.

Asiatic black bear rescue. The work of the Animals Asia Foundation (see www.animalsasia.org) also involves convincing people to use alternative medicines to the Asiatic black bear bile.

A last chance?

Most large zoos do more than simply display animals. Many of them have programs for breeding and reintroducing rare animals back into the wild. Many botanical gardens collect, store, and grow rare plant varieties so that they will not be lost forever.

CAPTIVE BREEDING

One of the leading centers for captive breeding in the world is Jersey Zoo in the Channel Islands. This zoo—which was set up by Gerald Durrell—breeds many endangered animals, such as the ring-tailed lemur and the aye-aye. San Diego Zoo's Wild Animal Park also runs breeding programs. For example, it has helped to increase the California Condor population from 25 in 1983 to 242 in June 2004. Captive breeding ensures that even if a species dies out in the wild, it will not become extinct.

Jersey Zoo has helped to run a captive breeding program for the echo parakeet in the bird's native home, the island of Mauritius. The zoo also runs an education program to teach people about the threats facing this bird and many other endangered animals.

REINTRODUCTION

The aim of captive breeding in many zoos is to reintroduce animals into the wild. For example, in Australia, the Tasmanian National Parks and Wildlife Service has been running a project to reintroduce the orange-bellied parrot. There are only a few hundred of these birds left in the wild.

This baby parrot is being hand-fed. The only way to save some endangered species is to breed them in controlled conditions, where they can grow in safety. When this bird is old enough, it will be released into the wild.

Action stations

The golden lion tamarin is threatened by the destruction of its home in the coastal forests of Brazil. Pockets of forest have been protected, and more than 100 zoos around the world have worked together to breed the golden lion tamarin in captivity. In recent years, more than 140 animals have been released into the wild. This strategy seems to be working: the golden lion tamarin population in the wild has risen from about 200 to more than 1,000.

The golden lion tamarin is found only in the lowland coastal forests of Brazil.

Panda protection

The giant panda is the symbol of the world's largest independent conservation organization—the WWF. The protection and conservation of the giant panda highlights many of the main issues that affect almost all endangered species.

PANDAS IN PERIL

There are now only about 1,600 giant pandas in the wild. Giant pandas are threatened by the same problems that affect almost all endangered wildlife: habitat destruction and poaching. Their forest homes in the mountain regions of southwest China have been heavily logged and cleared for farming. Now, many giant pandas live in small areas of bamboo vegetation little more than a mile wide.

Giant pandas are threatened by the loss of bamboo forests and by poaching. This giant panda cub was rescued after its mother was killed.

Action stations

Every year, the WWF holds a "Walk for Wildlife." In 2001 (WWF's 40th birthday), it raised money for giant panda projects in China. The group—the first international conservation organization to work in China—used the money to fund research, training, education, and the practical management of giant panda reserves.

Vets in China examine a giant panda as part of a captive breeding program. The WWF has many projects that help protect giant pandas.

HABITAT HELP

To protect giant pandas, the Chinese government has created a number of protected reserves and has banned logging in some areas where giant pandas live. However, giant pandas still are killed illegally, and more needs to be done to save them. One proposal is the development of more "bamboo corridors" to link areas where giant pandas live so that they can move around to eat and breed more easily.

People and wildlife

Almost everything we do has some effect on the plants and animals around us. One of the greatest challenges we face is finding ways to share the planet with the wildlife that lives here.

ENVIRONMENTALLY FRIENDLY PEOPLE

In many countries, people are becoming more aware of the environment. They are starting to change the way they do things, such as traveling, shopping, and working, so that they have less environmental impact. Some farsighted companies are also striving to become environmentally friendly by reducing the effect their factories and products have on wildlife.

In Madagascar, local people are trained as wildlife guides to show tourists their country's endangered wildlife.

Action stations

One of the best ways to get involved in the fight to save wildlife is to join an organization such as the WWF. If you are interested in one particular animal—such as the dolphin—you will almost certainly be able to join a specific group. As a member, you will be able to help the group raise money and get involved in its work.

These volunteers are hard at work clearing garbage from a towpath along a canal— an important man-made habitat for waterbirds and other animals.

PROTECTING BIODIVERSITY

Many governments are helping people save wildlife by creating laws and initiatives that protect areas where endangered plants and animals grow and live. Some action plans aim to conserve the number of species living in a particular area—its biodiversity. But such plans will work only if everyone plays a part. If we do not, the world will lose many more wonderful plants and animals.

Glossary

Biodiversity The variety of different species of living things that exist in a given area.

Botanical garden A place where a large number of different species of plants are grown. Botanical gardens are often open to the public.

Carbon dioxide The major greenhouse gas. Carbon dioxide occurs naturally but is also produced when fossil fuels such as oil, coal, and gas are burned.

Coral A marine creature that lives in warm seas. Coral has a skeleton of calcium carbonate (lime). As coral dies, these skeletons gradually form reefs that are home to a variety of marine wildlife.

Ecotourism A type of vacation designed to have little impact on the environment.

Environmentally friendly A product or activity that has as little environmental impact as possible or that helps protect, restore, or conserve the environment.

Extinction The complete disappearance of a species from the planet.

Food chain The eating order in nature, usually starting with plants and ending with meat-eating animals.

Gallbladder A small sac that is part of the digestive system. The gallbladder stores bile from the liver, where it is produced as part of the digestive process.

Global warming The gradual rise in Earth's temperature.

Greenhouse gases The gases that are thought by many scientists to be causing global warming. The main ones are carbon dioxide and methane.

Habitat The place where a plant or animal lives.

Organic Organic farming uses no man-made chemicals. Instead, natural products, such as animal waste, are used to make crops grow stronger.

Poacher A person who hunts, traps, or kills an animal illegally.

Persistent Organic Pollutants (POPs) Long-lasting, hazardous chemicals that are used in a number of industrial processes and that can be produced when garbage is burned.

Reintroduction The process in which a species of plant or animal is put back into a habitat from which it has disappeared.

Species A group of plants or animals that are very similar to each other and can reproduce together.

Tropical rain forest A type of forest that is usually found near the equator where it is hot and wet.

World Wildlife Fund (WWF) One of the world's leading environmental groups that campaigns for the protection of wildlife and its habitats.

Zoo A place where animals are kept in captivity for the public to see. Many carry out breeding programs and conservation awareness programs.

Find out more

www.cites.org
Find out all about CITES and take a look at the species database to see which animals are endangered.

www.endangeredearth.com
This site is a global source of information about the world's endangered animals. You can view pictures of several different endangered species.

www.greenpeace.org
Visit this site to find out about Greenpeace and its campaigns to conserve wildlife and the habitats in which it lives.

www.itdg.org
Learn about projects in the developing world that are helping people escape from poverty so that they can look after the environment more easily.

www.panda.org
The WWF's Web site contains a range of information about endangered species. Click on the "species" link to find out what is being done to conserve the world's rarest animals.

www.wdcs.org
Find out all about the protection of whales and dolphins at the site of the world's most active charity dedicated to their conservation and welfare.

Index